MW01489328

WOULD YOU LIKE FREE RESOURCES?

EMAIL "FREE" TO DECODABLETEXTS@GMAIL.COM TO SIGN UP FOR OUR NEWSLETTER AND RECEIVE FREE RESOURCES.

★ ★ ★ ★ ★

PLEASE CONSIDER LEAVING A REVIEW ON
AMAZON IF YOU LIKED THIS BOOK!

TABLE OF CONTENTS

CONSONANT BLENDS-SP

The Spud

Spack the spud liked to splash in the spa. He spun and splashed, making big splashes of water. He spent all day at the spa, getting lots of sun. He **spied** a little fish **swimming** by. Spack was so happy, he even let out a big spit of water. He was having a spiffy time at the spa.

Sally the Spider

Sally was a small spider. She was black and small. She saw a small spot. The spot was on a **leaf**. Sally wanted to spin a web on the spot. She spun a web on the spot. The web was small but **strong**. Sally saw a small **snail**. The snail was on the spot too. Sally said "snap snap" to the snail. The snail was scared and slid away. Sally was happy. She slept in her small web."

Spens

Spens likes to **grow** spuds. He had a spa for them. He would check the spots to see if they were **growing** well. The spuds were big. He would look at them all. He would then pick them up and **bring** them in. He would then spun them and make spud chips. Spens likes to eat them with some spam. He spent all day tending to his spuds. He even put a spec of salt on them to make them extra good.

The Spiders Journey

There were two spiders **named** Spot and Span. They **lived** in a big, old house. They spent their days spinning webs. They were fast spinners. Spot was **faster** than Span. They would **race** each other to see who could spin the best web. They would end up having fun. They had a big spider family that they spent time with. But one day, they wanted to see the world. They spent days planning the trip and packing bags. They set off on their **journey** and had many good **times.** But the best part was that they could always count on each other and their strong, spun webs to keep them safe.

The Nest

Sparrow was a **busy** body. She had to get the best spot to **make** her nest. She went and looked for the best spot. She **saw** a spot in a big tree. She span twigs and grass to make her nest. She spent all day spinning it. It was a good nest. She was so **proud** of it. She would spit out any twig that was not right. She made sure it was the best nest. She laid her eggs in the nest. They were speckled and brown. She would watch over them and make sure they were **safe**. The nest was the best place for her to spend time with her family.

A New Toy

The **sparrow** flew by the trees. She spotted a **spoon** on a branch. She flew over and used her wing to **spear** the spoon. She flew back to her nest and spent time playing with her new spoon. She spun it, flipped it, and even tried to put it on her beak. She was so happy with her new spoon, she sang a song of thanks. The other sparrows by her speckled her with weird looks.

CONSONANT BLENDS- ST

My Stuff

My stuff is with the staff. My stuff is still on the stand. My stuff is full of stocks and sticks. My stuff is cool. My stuff is still. My stuff is full of stamps. My stuff is stuck. My stuff is stacked. I love my stuff.

Still

I stand still. I stand still on the hill. I stand still like I am stuck. But I am not stuck. Mom said to stand like a stack of sticks. It stunk on the hill. But I do not stomp. I do not step. I do not stop. I stand still on this hill. I stand still like I am stunned.

Stuck

The stag was stuck in the stem of a tree. He went to step, but he could not. He asked the staff for help. But they did not. He went to step and stunt from the tree. But he was not skilled at stepping. A kind man walked by and saw him. The man pulled and pulled. He freed the stag from the stem. The stag was so happy and thanked the man. Then, he ran into the forest.

The Stork's Meal

The stork stood still on the stump. It was a big, strong stork. It had a big, fluffy head of **feathers** and a long, skinny neck. The stork would stand on one leg and study the people, bugs, and animals. It was looking for something to eat, but it was picky. It only wanted the freshest bugs and **worms**. One day, the stork spotted a big worm. It quickly went **down** and snatched it up. The stork held on tight. It was a tasty treat for the stork, who flew away to find more food

The Ride of a Lifetime

The stop **sign** was red. The kids had to stop the bike. They saw a star in the sky. They wanted to stab at it with a stick. But it was too **high**. They saw a stub and they stepped on it. They heard a stem snap. They were stunned. They saw a stag in the bushes. It was still and **staring** at them. They started to stand up. The stag ran into the trees. They saw a stock of berries. They ate them and felt stuffed. They stamped on the ground. They had a stint of fun **before** they had to go home.

The Spaceman

Once upon a time, a little boy wanted to go to **space**. He spent all his time looking at the **stars** and the planets. He could not stop looking. He made rocket. He stepped onto the rocket. He said, "3, 2, 1, Blast off!" His rocket went into the sky and into the stars. The boy could not believe it. He was stunned! He was in space! He wanted to stay still with the stars. He wanted to stand as tall as the sun. Space was beautiful.

CONSONANT BLENDS-CR

Crazy

I am not crazy. I like crust. I like to crash into the wall. I like crickets. I can be cranky. But I am not crazy. I like credit for being good. I like to crunch my drinks. I like to craft things then crush them. But I am not crazy.

Crabs

The crab is by the crop. He is in the crud. A crab is by the crib. A crab crosses the crisp red grass. The crabs are crazy. The crabs get into so much crunchy nonsense. But the crabs are pretty.

Crab Fight

Once upon a time, there was a little crab who lived by the **sea**. He loved to crunch on sea plants. One day, he sw that his crop of sea plants were **gone**. He cried and cried, but no one came to help. He **decided** to take matters into his own claws. He set out to find the culprit. He looked over the rocky cliffs. He found the big crab who had taken his plants. The little crab **stood** up to the big crab. He said, "This is my crop! Leave it!" The big crab was so **surprised** that he dropped the plants and ran away. The little crab was happy and took his plants back to his crib.

The Sauce

Once upon a time, there was a **farmer** who had a big crop of **tomatoes**. He was so happy with his crop that he cried. He put the tomatoes in a crib to keep them safe. But then, a big **storm** came and the wind whipped across the land. All the tomatoes fell out of the crib and were crushed. The farmer was so sad, he wanted to cry again. He saw a crab crawling on the ground and thought it was a bad omen. He thought, "this is just a crap day." He went to bed sad. But when he **woke** up, he saw that the tomatoes had cracked open and were now **tasty**. He had the best idea to craft them into **tomato sauce.** He sold the tomato sauce to pay off his credit. He lived happily ever after.

Crunch to the Rescue

Once there was a cat named Crunch. He loved to play with his friends. His best friend was a little crab named Crump. They would play all day, running and having fun. But one day, Crunch heard a crash. He went to it and saw that a big storm had **knocked** down a bunch of branches from a tree. Crunch knew he had to help his friend Crump. So he went to the branches to find him. But Crump was stuck and crying for help. Crunch used all his strength to move the branches and free his friend. Crump was so thankful and thanked Crunch for being such a good friend. From then on, they made sure to play in safe spots.

Chris the Strong

There was once a little boy named Chris. He had a bully at school. He was sad and cried a lot. Chris was cross. But one day, he wanted to stand up for himself. His **teacher** said to "never give up and to keep trying." This was his new crest. He made a craft project to stop the bully. He told his parents. He even wrote a **letter** to the teachers about the bullying. In the end, the bully was sorry and Chris was no longer cross. Chris felt a crisp sense of joy.

CONSONANT BLENDS- DR

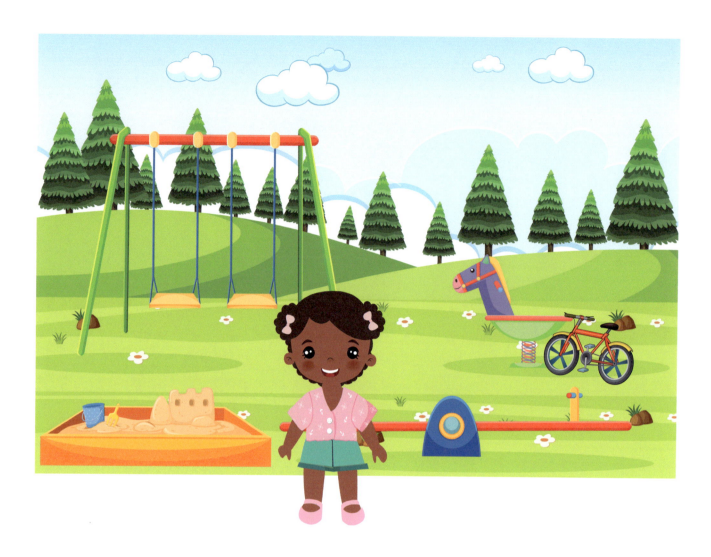

The Good Day

I hit the drum. It was a bit drab. I put on the dress. I did not like it. I drift on my bike. I try but it is too dry. I drop my bike in the grass. I drank water. It dripped and spilled. It is a good day.

The Drag Race

The day was drab. The cars were set to drag **race**. The red car pulled off like a drum. "Drink my dust," the driver said to the rest of the cars. But the red car dripped liquid from behind. Without much happening, the red car driffted into the tree. The red car was dry because it dripped all of it's gas. The rest of the cars had not drank the red car's dust. They kept on in the race. The driver of the red car now knew, he should not say such things before winning. The driver got a drill and gas and began to fix his car. He dragged his car to the side but the race was over. He lost, but learned a good lesson.

Drib the Dragon

Once upon a time, there was a dragon named Drib. He loved to drop by the water and get a drip to drink. He would often **draw** in the sand and play his dragon drum. One day, Drib went for a drink. As he was taking a drink, he saw a woman in a red dress. He drifted and took a look. The woman in the red dress asked for help. The woman said that she had been kidnapped by an evil witch who had put a spell on her. Drib knew he had to help. He quickly came up with a plan to drag the witch out of her **castle** and put an end to her evil. With the help of his drums and dragon drill, Drib and the woman beat the witch. From that day on, the woman and Drib were friends.

The Bear and the Fox

One day, the bear fell upon a **river** and drank from it. The fox watched, then snuck to the river and drank from it as well. They both felt good and sat in the sun, letting the day drift by. Then, the fox heard a drill. He jumped up and told the bear, who was driven to act. It was a **hunter**. They both quickly dressed in grass and sticks. They wanted to blend in with the forest. The hunter walked right by them. But he did not see them. Just then, the bear dropped a drum and jumped up. He **scared** the hunter. The hunter ran out of the drab forest. The bear and the fox let the days drift by.

The Warning Call

A **dolphin** and a **whale** lived in the sea. Their names were Drat and Drit. The dolphin, Drat, loved to play in the waves. The Whale, Drit, was content to drift and watch. One day, drat spotted a fishing **boat** with a big drill. It was going to be bad for the animals. The whale was driven to act and made a **warning** call. A deep drum sound went in all the sea. Drit and Drat dressed in seaweed and shells to blend in with the sea floor. The fishing boat drifted by. They did not see Drat and Drit. Drat and Drit drifted off, thankful for each other's quick thinking.

CONSONANT BLENDS-TR

The Track

The trip was good. It was to the track. The trip was full of tricks. It had the best trends. I had to trust my mom on the trip. It was a long treck. But the trip's tricks gave me the biggest **smile**.

Track

Track wanted to try extra **hard** in her new job as a traffic boss. She knew the job was **hard**. She had to have strict control of the metro **streets**. But with her trusty trident in hand, and her retro jacket, she felt confident. She trusted her skills. As she went up the streets, she saw a truck stuck on the road. Track acted quickly. She set up her traffic traps and made the cars go away. Thanks to her quick thinking and strong skills, she was trusted.

The Trap

There was a girl named Trin. She wanted to try extra hard to pass a test. She set a trap. If Trin did not study, the trap made her trip. Trin **studied** on the weekends. She trusted her plan. But one day, she took a trip to the retro city. She got lost in the trash. She got lost on the metro. But Trin was strong. She took control. She went with traffic to find her way back to her house. Trin had to study quickly before her trap tripped her. Trin passed her test. Her trap did not go off.

Sam the Driver

There was a truck **driver** named Tricksy. He was a good driver. But he wanted to try something extra. One day, he got a new truck that could travel on tricky **roads**. Tricksy wanted to give it a try. He took a trip to get one. He liked the truck's trim. Tricksy got the truck. Tricksy took the truck on a trip. He packed his bags, set the G.P.S. and hit the road. But he did not know that the truck had a hidden defect. It had a bad trap which made the truck drift. Tricksy had to think quick as the truck drifted. He was able to get to the next stop. He got the truck fixed. Tricksy went extra quick back to his home.

The Brave Astronaut

Once upon a time, a brave **astronaut** named Tristin wanted to travel to a distant planet. He had to be extra **careful** not to get trapped on the planet. His ship had all the best stuff. He had a retro control pad. As he went into **space**, he saw traffic from comits and had to use his trusty ship's controls to go **through** it. He had to make a quick trip to the trash bin to get rid of any bad **equipment**. But when he got to the planet, he realized that his ship's gas was low. He had to think fast and come up with a trick to extend his ship's gas. He began to eject any trash out of the ship he did not **need**. This helped the ship get back home.

The Farm and the Farmer

There was a **farmer** named **Trudy**. She tried extra hard to grow the best crops. She set traps for pests, took trips to the city to buy new **seeds**, and picked up trash in the trench. But one day, a strong storm **caused** a lot of **damage** to the farm. Trudy knew she had to take control. She called for help from her **friends** to fix the farm. Trudy went to clean up the track. She trimmed the grass. She trusted her friends and they helped her. They even got a truck to get up the trash. With their hard work, they got the farm back to **normal**.

CONSONANT BLENDS- GR AND BR

Hard Work

Gramps was on the go. He would grab his broom and bring a water for his brisk walk. One day, he saw a bracket of **paper** and wanted to grant himself a grin. He gripped the bracket and gave it a grind, but it was too hard. Gramps did not give up. He **showed** his grit and **broke** the bracket. It took a grand effort. In the end, Gramps had a grand time, and he was happy with his work.

Grands Camp Trip

Gramps and Brad went on a camp trip. They had a grill and grilled some grub for lunch. Brad grabbed the water and Gramps grinned. They sat on the brink of the lake and watched the sun set with a brisk **breeze**. Then, they went to the tent to get some rest. Brad had a good grip on their blankets. In the morning, they went for a walk and came across a grand tree. Gramps used his grit and made the climb up to the top with Brad's help. They then had a grand time picking fresh apples. Gramps and Brad had a grand time.

Basketball Brad

Brad and his friends loved to play basketball. They would grin as they **dribble** the ball and made shots. Brad jumped and grabbed the ball. He would brag to his friends about his skills. One day, the ball got stuck in a bracket on the wall. Brad tried to grasp it with his hands. But it was too high. Then, his friend Griff came with a broken broom. They used it to **knock** the ball down and Brad grabbed it. The other kids were happy and Brad could not help but grin. They all had a brisk and fun time playing basketball together.

CONSONANT BLENDS- STR AND SCR

The Bird Trap

The scrappy cats strung up a scrap of string from the bird **feeder** to a tree branch. This made a trap for the birds in a tree. They watched as the birds scratched and scruffed at the seed. They did not know of the cats' strict plan. But the birds were strong, and one by one, they stretched and stripped the string. The birds did not stress. The birds got away. The cats were upset. The cats were hungry. But the cats were strong. The cats knew they could get food **later**.

The Scrap Car

In an odd **world**, cars talked. Shiny strapped cars strummed and strutted on the streets. But one car named Stram, a messed-up old scrap car, was odd. It had strong **tires** and could take a lot of stress. The strict traffic **laws** were stressful for the scrap car Stram. It was odd to see among the strata of cars. The scrap car was **able** to strum its way in the city, talking with cars and making friends. Strum met two cars. Scram and Scrim. All the cars went across the streets. All the cars were strong and scrappy. All the cars were happy.

Space Dogs

The alien dogs landed on the **strange** planet. The dog's fur was scrappy and scruffy. They went around the planet, trying to think of a plan. One dog, with a strong and strict **voice**, said "We must scrape and scrimp for food if we're going to live on this planet." Then, a big dog named Stramp, with a strap on his back, said "we should try to strap all the dogs to the planet's animals. We will get on top of them and travel to find food." So they all strung together a crude strap and set off on the strange planet. The animal stroll was hard. Even with the dogs traveling on top of other animals, it tested their strength. Each dog wanted to scratch their head, scrub their belly, and give up. At last, the dogs saw food and **water**. The dogs were happy.

The Best Goats Ever

The goats on the **farm** were a scrappy bunch. They would often scruff up their fur and scrunch. Some scratched an itch. They loved to strut up and down the farm. Their strong legs strolled on the track. They ran as if a wolf said scram. The farmer had to be strict with them. He wanted to make sure they did not go too far and get into **trouble**. But the goats were playful, and loved to play games of tag. They would often scrimp along the farm, trying to find a way to sneak a peek at the farm next **door**. But the farmer kept a close watch, making sure his goats were always safe.

The Scroll

The boys strutted down the street with their scrap of **paper** in hand. They were scruffy and scrappy, but they had a plan to scrunch the paper and make a scroll. The scroll was a new script. They soon had a script **ready** and they went off to make their script a play. They yelled and threw the scrap paper, making it look like it was raining. The **actors** picked up the script. The scrappy cast was **ready**. The boys had a good time. The scrappy actors had a good time. The play went from scratch paper to a big, good time.

CONSONANT BLENDS- THR AND TW

The Job

The three of us, twin brothers, and our thrifty father, set out to fix our old house. We thrust into the tasks, throwing out the trash and scrubbing the floors. We twisted and **turned** to reach every nook and cranny. My body throbbed from the work. Though the work was hard, the thrill of tasks kept us going. It was a thrill. We thrash and twist out all the trash in the house. We even **found** a few thrifty, hidden away riches. We found a twin set of beds. In the end, our hard work **paid** off as the house looked brand new.

Mom's Party

The twins threw a **party** for their mom. She was twenty-seven. They had thrifted fun things to put up for the party. They used twisted twigs and a few thrifty finds. Throngs of **people** came and were thrilled to be a **part** of the party. The party was a big hit. The music made the people want to thrust and twist on the **dance floor**. The twin's mom was thrown into a fit of joy. The thrills of the party made her happy. As the night went on, the people at the party twanged and twitched to the music. It was a happy day.

The Safari Ride

The three of us set off on a thrilling safari ride. We thrust into the African Savanna. We were thrown into a throng of wild animals. Each one was a thrall to the African **forest**. Our **guide**, a strict and thrifty man, led us through the thickets with a twig in hand. He pointed out twin zebras and twenty or so twitching lions. As we twisted and turned through the savanna, the thrill of the ride was in the air. We were between the lions and the elephants, but the fun was nonstop. We could not wait for the next twist and twang of our **journey**.

Paris

In Paris, the twins twirled in the streets. Their eyes wide with happiness. The **Eiffel Tower** thrust into the sky, which made them twitch with thrills. The throngs of people thrown together in the streets made a constant thrum of energy. They twisted and turned. Taking in the sights and sounds, and even managed to find a thrifty food truck. The city had the twins thrust under its **thrall**. As the sun set, they threw their arms **around** each other, knowing this trip was a once in a **lifetime** twist of fate.

thank you

Dear Friends,

Thank you for choosing our book. I hope that this book serves you and your family well. If you have found value in this book, please consider leaving us a review on amazon. It would be very much appreciated.

Adam Freeman

Here is a suggested order to teach beginning reading skills.

Short Vowel Sounds

Digraphs

Consonant Blends

Word Endings— s, ed, ing.

Silent E

Vowel Teams

Controlled R

Made in the USA
Columbia, SC
22 April 2025

57028380R00031